# ALVIN
## AND
# THE CHIPMUNKS™

# JOKE BOOK
## 100+ JOKES!

By
Kirsten
Mayer

Scholastic Inc.

Interior design by Kay Petronio
Cover design by Cheung Tai

Text © 2012 by Scholastic Inc.
All rights reserved. Published by Scholastic Inc.
SCHOLASTIC and associated logos are trademarks and/or
registered trademarks of Scholastic Inc.

12 11 10 9 8                                        16

ISBN 978-0-545-48121-2

Printed in the U.S.A    40
First printing, September 2012

# CONTENTS

# GOING NUTTY

How do you make a
walnut laugh?
**Crack it up!**

What do you call
a pistachio in a
spacesuit?
**An astronut!**

Why did the chipmunk cross the road?
**To get his nut to the other side!**

What do you call a pirate obsessed with finding a treasure chest?
**A chestnut!**

What did Alvin call his scary dream about an acorn?
**A *nutmare!***

What kind of shoes do millionaires wear?

**Cashews!**

How do you catch a chipmunk?

**Climb into a tree and act like a nut.**

Why does the chipmunk think he's crazy?

**Because someone told him, "you are what you eat," and he only eats nuts!**

What's that joke about peanut butter?

**I'm not telling you. You might spread it!**

Why did the girl love hot chocolate?

**Because she was a cocoanut!**

What kind of nuts pop?

**A-corns!**

What do you call a nut
who likes to play chess?
**A chess-nut!**

What kind of nuts always
have colds?
**Cashews!**

What two nuts went out on a date?
**Al Mond and
Hazel Nut.**

What nut is a vegetable?
**A pea-nut.**

Why did the fisherman put peanut butter on his fishing pole?
**He was trying to catch a jellyfish!**

Knock, knock!
**Who's there?**
Cash.
**Cash who?**
No thanks. I prefer peanuts to cashews.

Knock, knock!
**Who's there?**
Pecan.
**Pecan who?**
Pecan someone your
own size!

Knock, knock!
**Who's there?**
Ice cream soda.
**Ice cream soda
who?**
Ice cream soda whole
world will know
what a nut you are!

# THAT TASTES FUNNY

What does it mean if you've got melted chocolate all over your hands?

**That you're eating it too slowly.**

What kind of keys do kids prefer over house keys?

**Cookies!**

What do you call cheese that isn't yours?
**Nacho cheese!**

Why do the French eat snails?
**Because they don't like fast food!**

What's Alvin's favorite number when he's hungry?
**Ate!**

What do you call a pig that does karate?
**A pork chop!**

How much do pirates pay for corn?
**A buccaneer!**

Why shouldn't we tell an egg any of these jokes?
**Why? Because it might crack up!**

What did the baby corn say to the mom corn?
**Where is Pop corn?**

Why didn't the melons get married?

**Because they cantaloupe!**

Why did the banana go to the doctor?

**Because it wasn't peeling well!**

Why shouldn't you tell a secret on a farm?

**Because the potatoes have eyes and the corn have ears!**

What is a pretzel's favorite dance?
**The twist!**

What kind of fruit do twins like to eat?
**Pears!**

What do you call a shivering cow?
**Beef jerky!**

Why did Alvin invite the mushroom to his birthday party?
**Because he's a fungi!**

What do you give to a sick lemon?
**Lemon aid!**

When was the pepper being nosy?
**When it was jalapeño business!**

What do you call a monkey that eats potato chips?
**A chipmunk.**

A man ordered coffee in a diner. He took a sip and then called over the waiter. "Excuse me, this coffee tastes like mud."

"yes, sir," said the waiter. "It's fresh ground."

Two muffins are sitting in the oven, baking. One muffin says to the other, "Man, it's hot in here!"

**The other muffin points and says, "HEY, LOOK! A TALKING MUFFIN!"**

Knock, knock!
**Who's there?**
Bacon.
**Bacon who?**
Bacon a cake for your birthday!

Knock, knock!
**Who's there?**
Gorilla.
**Gorilla who?**
Gorilla up some steaks! I'm starving!

# ROCKIN' SOME LAUGHS

What type of music
scares balloons?
**Pop music!**

How do you wear music on
your head?
**Wear a headband!**

How does the turkey play music?

**He uses his drumsticks!**

What is the difference between a fish and a piano?

**You can't tune a fish!**

Why are fish so good at practicing music?
**They already know their scales.**

Why did the girl go up to the roof to sing?
**She wanted to reach the high notes!**

What kind of music do mummies listen to?
**Wrap music!**

How do you fix a broken tuba?
**With a tuba glue!**

Why did the hummingbird hum?
**It forgot the words!**

Which composer is a chicken's favorite?

**Bach, Bach, Bach!**

Why should you keep your CDs in the refrigerator?

**Because then they will be really cool!**

What's a chipmunk's favorite type of music?

**'Munk and roll!**

Knock, knock!

**Who's there?**

A little old lady.

**A little old lady who?**

I didn't know you could yodel.

# UP A TREE

What did the chipmunk say to the tree?

**It's been nice gnawing you!**

Why did the leaf go to the doctor?

**It was green!**

What is a tree's least favorite month?
**Sep-timber!**

What did the tree wear to the pool party?
**Swimming trunks!**

What's the best way to carve a stick?
**Whittle by whittle!**

What kind of tree can fit into your hand?
**A palm tree!**

How do trees get on the Internet?
**They log on.**

What did the one stick say to the other stick at the party?
**Let's make like trees and leave!**

TEAM MUNK

TEAM MUNK

25

Why was the tree sent to its room?
**Because it was being knotty!**

Why was the tree drooling?
**It was a dogwood.**

Knock, knock!
**Who's there?**
Leaf.
**Leaf who?**
Leaf me alone already!

# FUN IN THE SUN

What did the elephant wear at the beach?
**Swimming trunks!**

How did the fish show their appreciation
for the song?
**They did the wave!**

Why was the
whale so sad?
**He was a
blue whale.**

What did the captain do with his sick boat?
**He took it to the dock!**

Why did the dolphin cross the ocean?
**To get to the other tide.**

Why didn't the shrimp share his treasure?
**Because he was a little shellfish!**

What kind of fish could you use in the winter?
**Skate!**

Why did the elephant get kicked out of the pool?
**He kept dropping his trunks!**

Who stars in a concert at the beach?
**The starfish!**

Who's the ruler of the beach?
**The king crab!**

Why do some fish live in salt water?
**Because they are allergic to pepper!**

What washes up on tiny beaches?
**Microwaves!**

What do sharks say when something radical happens?
**Jawesome!**

What kind of socks do pirates wear?
**Arrrrrgyle!**

What do frogs drink on hot summer days?
**Croak-a-cola!**

What did the pirate say when his wooden leg got stuck in the freezer?
**Shiver me timbers!**

Which fish is the richest?
**The goldfish!**

Knock, knock!
**Who's there?**
Yacht.
**Yacht who?**
Yacht to know who I am
by now!

Knock, knock!
**Who's there**
Yachts.
**Yachts who?**
Yachts up, doc?

Knock, knock!

**Who's there?**

Water.

**Water who?**

Water you doing? Open the door!

Knock, knock!

**Who's there?**

Island.

**Island who?**

Island on your roof with a
hang-glider!

# PLAYING AROUND

What do you call a boomerang that never comes back?

**A stick.**

What's a cheerleader's favorite color?

**yeller!**

Why do basketball players love donuts?

**Because they can dunk them!**

How do basketball players stay cool?

**They sit next to the fans.**

What's the difference between a baby and a basketball player?

**One drools and the other dribbles!**

How is a baseball team like a pancake?

**They both need a good batter!**

Why did Cinderella get kicked off of the basketball team?

**Because she ran away from the ball!**

What is harder to catch the faster you run?
**your breath!**

Why did the coach go to the bank?
**To get his quarterback.**

Why did the golfer bring two pairs of pants to the game?
**In case he got a hole in one!**

How do chipmunks win a trophy?
**By winning a ChampionChip game!**

What's Alvin's favorite position on the football team?
**Quartermunk!**

# WACKY WINTER

Where do snowmen
keep their money?
**In snowbanks!**

What do you get if you
cross an apple with a
Christmas tree?
**A pineapple!**

What do snowmen wear on their heads?
**Ice caps!**

What sort of ball doesn't bounce?
**A snowball!**

What do you get if you give a snowman teeth?
**Frostbite!**

What do you call a snowman in the summer?
**A puddle.**

What does a snowman do when he's mad?
**He gives you the cold shoulder.**

Where do you train sled dogs?
**In a mush room!**

What did one snowman say to the other snowman?

**Do you smell carrots?**

What do chipmunks say to each other at the holidays?

**Merry Chipmas!**

What do Spanish chipmunks say?

**Furries Navidad!**

Knock, knock!

**Who's there?**

Alvin.

**Alvin who?**

Alvinlanche! Ruuuuuun!

Knock, knock!

**Who's there?**

Yule.

**Yule who?**

Yule never know!

# JUST FOR FUN!

Knock, knock!
**Who's there?**
Never.
**Never who?**
Never mind.

Someone said you sound like an owl?
**WHOOOO?**

What do you call an alligator in a vest?
**An investigator!**

What do you get when you cross a T. rex with fireworks?
**Dino-mite!**

Why shouldn't you write with a broken pencil?
**Because it's pointless!**

When does Friday come before Thursday?
**In the dictionary!**

What did one hat say to the other hat?
**You stay here, I'll go on ahead!**

What do clouds wear under their shorts?
**Thunderpants!**

Knock, knock!
**Who's there?**
Cargo.
**Cargo who?**
Cargo beep beep!

What did the digital clock say to the grandfather clock?

**Look, Grandpa, no hands!**

What kind of flower is on your face?
**Tulips!**

What did 0 say
to 8?
**Nice belt!**

What has four
wheels and flies?
**A garbage
truck!**

Knock, knock!
**Who's there?**
Boo.
**Boo who?**
Don't cry, it's just a joke.

Knock, knock!

**Who's there?**

Woo!

**Woo who?**

Don't get so excited, it's just a joke!

Knock, knock!

**Who's there?**

Theodore!

**Theodore who?**

Theodore wasn't open so I knocked!

Knock, knock!

**Who's there?**

Venice.

**Venice who?**

Venice Dave going to be home???!